KU-424-929

Schools Library and Information Services
S00000685928

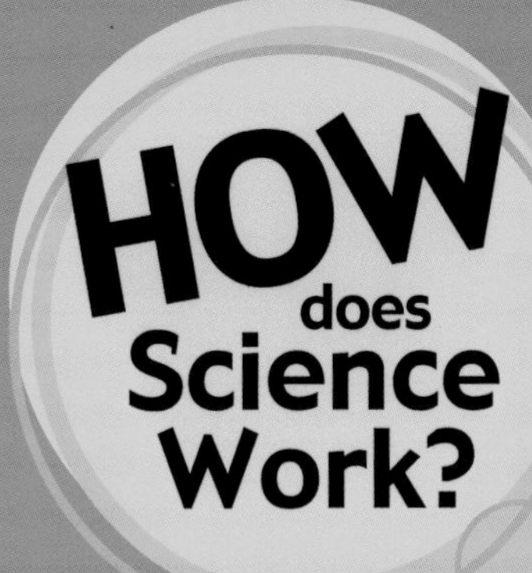

Light

written by
Carol Ballard

First published in Great Britain in 2006 by Wayland
An imprint of Hachette Children's Books

Hachette Children's Books
338 Euston Road, London NW1 3BH

Commissioning Editor: Vicky Brooker
Editors: Laura Milne, Camilla Lloyd
Senior Design Manager: Rosamund Saunders
Design and artwork: Peta Phipps
Commissioned Photography: Philip Wilkins
Consultant: Dr Peter Burrows
Series Consultant: Sally Hewitt
Artwork p.11: Peter Bull

Printed and bound in China

British Library Cataloguing in Publication Data
Ballard, Carol
Light. - (How does science work?)
1.Light - Juvenile literature
I.Title
535

ISBN-10 0-7502-4594-8
ISBN-13 978-0-7502-4594-4

Acknowledgements:

Cover photograph: A Rainbow over a Forest, Jeff Vanuga/Corbis

Photo credits: John Lamb/Getty Images 4, Chad Ehlers/Alamy 5, Charles Gullung/Getty Images 6, oote boe/Alamy 7, Martin Bond/Science Photo Library 8, Grace/Corbis 10, Paul Ridsdale/Alamy 18, Bsip/Chassenet Science Photo Library 19 both, Jerry Driendl/Getty Images 20, Heinrich van den Berg/Getty Images 21, Gary Crabbe/Alamy 22, Tom Robinson/Getty Images 24, Michael A. Keller/Corbis 26, Jeff Vanuga/Corbis 28.

The author and publisher would like to thank the models Dylan Chen and Kodie Briggs.

Contents

Words in **bold** can be found in the glossary on p.30

Light

Light is important to every living thing on Earth. Without light, our planet would be dark and dead. There would be no plants or animals.

We need light for everyday activities. It would be difficult to get washed and dressed and eat our meals without light. We need light for reading, writing, playing games and sports. Light is used in many different ways.

Light from the Sun lets these children see their football.

Lighthouses warn ships about the dangerous rocks.

Traffic signals help us to stay safe and flashing lights on emergency vehicles warn us to get out of the way. Televisions, cinemas and computers use light and help us to work and play. **Microscopes** use light to let us see very tiny things and **telescopes** let us see things far away. Light is really important.

Where does light come from?

Our most important **light source** is the Sun. Other stars are light sources too, but they do not look as big or as bright from Earth because they are further away. The Moon may look bright in the sky but it is not a light source – it only shines because light from the Sun bounces off it.

The Sun is a star, a huge ball of very hot gases, that gives our planet light and heat.

Never look directly at the Sun! It could damage your eyes.

A torch, candle or light bulb all give out light and are called light sources. Some light sources, such as the Sun or a fire, are natural sources. Other light sources, like a torch or a light bulb are **man-made**.

↑ **Street lights are used to light up dark streets.**

How does light travel?

Light travels away from the Sun in straight lines that spread out in every direction. Light travels very fast.

You can see the straight lines of sunlight shining between the trees.

TRY THIS! See how light travels

1 Find some hosing to use as your tube.

2 Hold a torch and shine it into the hosing.

3 Look down your tube.

4 Can you see the light from the torch?

5 Bend the hosing and look down the bent tube again.

6 Can you see the light from the torch?

You should find that, when the tube is straight, you can see the light from the torch. When the tube is bent you cannot see the light. This is because light cannot get round the bend in your tube.

Wow!

Light travels at an amazing speed – at 300,000 km every second. It is the fastest thing in the universe!

How do we see?

Our eyes let us see shapes, colours and movement in the world around us. It is light entering our eyes that makes our eyes work.

Look at your eyes in a **mirror**. What can you see? Eye lashes and eyebrows help to keep dust, dirt and sweat out of your eyes. The coloured ring is called the **iris**. The black dot in the centre is called the **pupil**. It is a hole through which light gets into your eye.

Your irises can be blue, grey, brown or green.

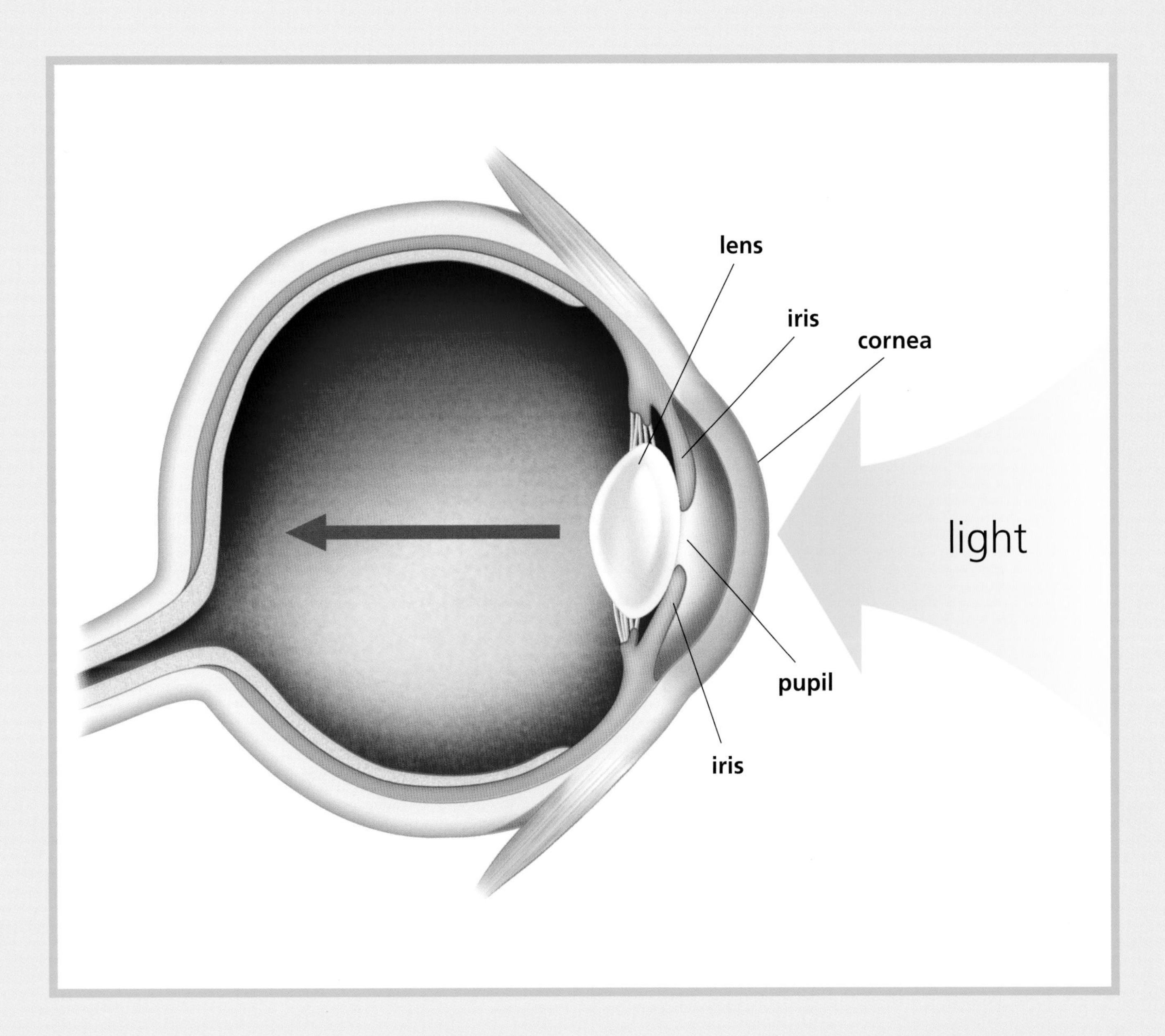

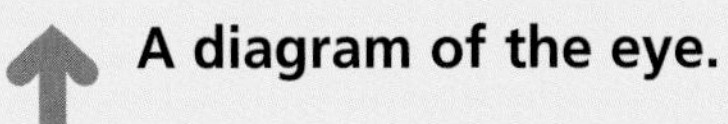
A diagram of the eye.

Light travels through the air to the eye. It travels through the clear covering of the eye called the **cornea**. Inside the eye, a jelly-like **lens** bends the light a little. The light travels to the back of the eye. The back of the eye sends messages to the brain. The brain gets the messages and works out what you are seeing.

Light and materials

Light can travel easily through materials like glass, clear plastic and water. Materials like this are called **transparent**. They are useful for making things you want to see through, like windows.

Materials that let only some light through are called **translucent**. Things look hazy or coloured if you look through them. Tracing paper, coloured glass and some plastics are like this.

These are made from transparent materials.

These are made from translucent materials.

Other materials like stone, wood and metals let no light through at all. You cannot see anything through them. They are called **opaque** materials. They are used to make things that you do not want to see through, such as walls and doors.

These are made from opaque materials.

Shadows

A **shadow** is made when an opaque object, like a wall or a tree, gets in the way of light. Light rays cannot travel through an opaque object. This means that there will be a dark area, that we call a shadow.

You can make animal shadows with your hands on the wall if there is a light shining behind you.

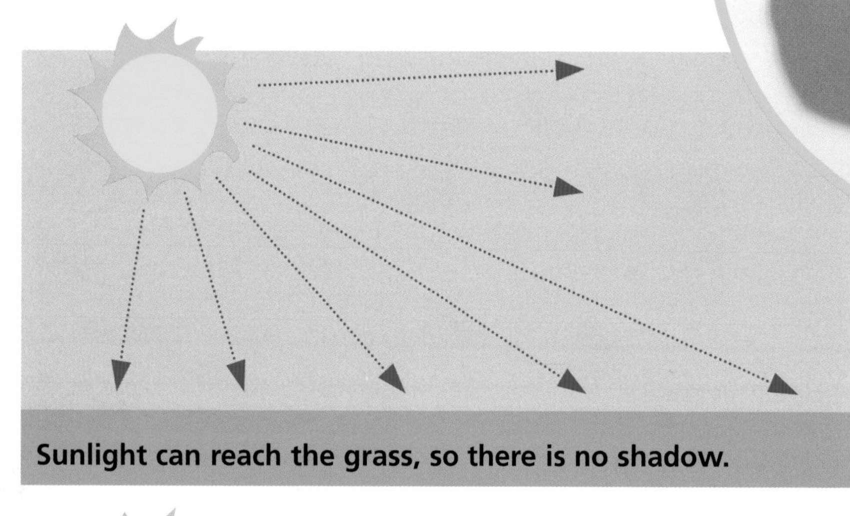

Sunlight can reach the grass, so there is no shadow.

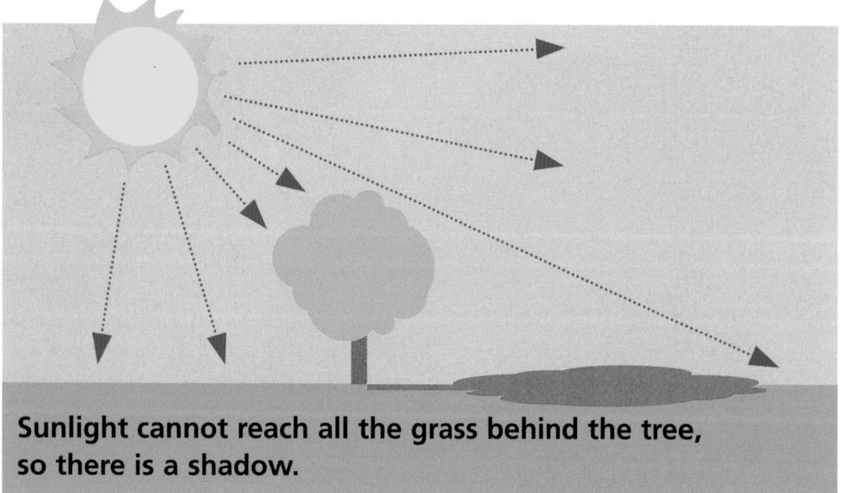

Sunlight cannot reach all the grass behind the tree, so there is a shadow.

TRY THIS! Watch shadows change size

1 Stand a toy in front of a wall.

2 Shine a torch at the toy so that it makes a shadow on the wall.

3 Move the torch closer to the toy.

4 What happens to the shadow?

5 Move the torch further away from the toy.

6 What happens to the shadow?

You could write your results in a table like this one.

Distance between torch and toy (in cm)	10	20	30	40	50
Height of shadow (in cm)	80	64	48	30	12

A bar chart would help you to show the information.

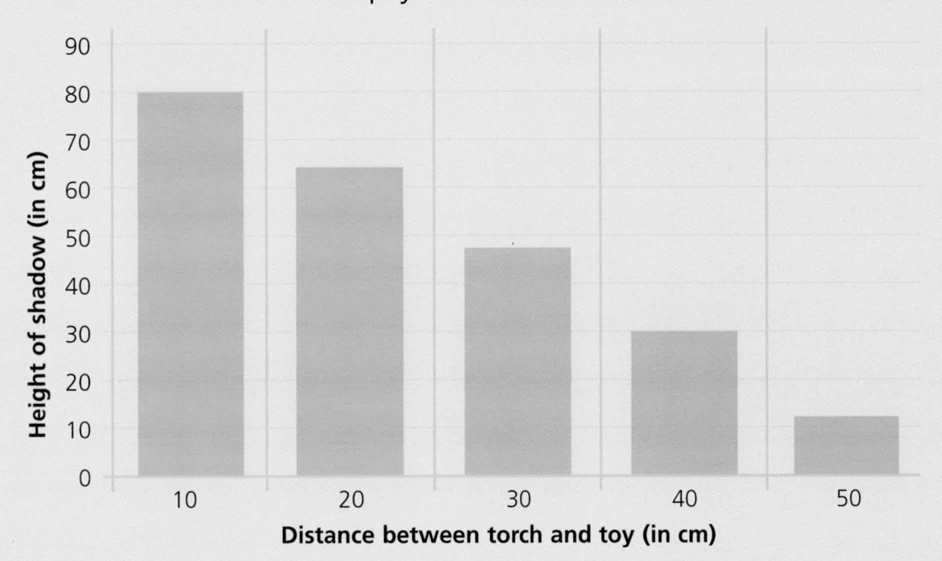

You should find that, the closer the torch is to the toy, the bigger the shadow.

Times of day

Have you ever noticed that your shadow seems to point in different directions at different times of day?

This happens because every day, as the Earth spins, the Sun's position in the sky changes. The Sun does not move, it just looks as if it does. The Sun is low and in the east in the morning. At midday, the Sun is high in the sky. By evening, the sun is low and in the west.

Long shadow in the morning.

Short shadow at midday.

Long shadow in the evening.

Can you see how the tree's shadow changes throughout the day?

TRY THIS! Watch shadows move

1. Use Blu-Tack or plasticine to stick a small container on the end of a stick.
2. Use some more Blu-Tack to fix your stick upright.
3. Position a light to one side of the container.
4. Draw round the shadow on a piece of paper.
5. Move the light straight above the container and draw round the shadow again.
6. Shine the light from the other side and draw round the shadow again.

Can you see how changing the light's position affects the shadow?

Wow!

As the Earth spins, each part faces the Sun and then faces away from it. This makes day and night.

In the dark

When there is no light, we say it is dark. We cannot see anything because no light enters our eyes.

We need to take special care when it is dark. Cars and bicycles use headlights and rear lights to see and be seen. Important road signs are lit up. Street lights help everyone to see where they are going.

If you ride a bicycle in the dark, make sure you are wearing reflective clothing to help you be seen by people in cars.

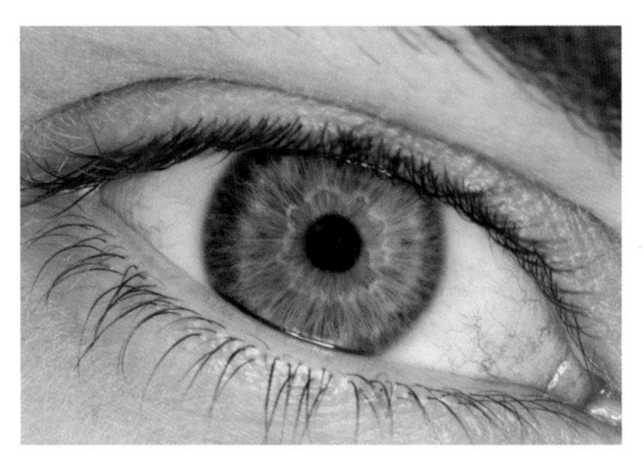

Your iris controls how much light enters your eye. In bright light, the iris muscles **contract**, making the pupil very small. This stops too much light entering the eye and damaging it. In dim light, the iris muscles **relax**, making the pupil very big.

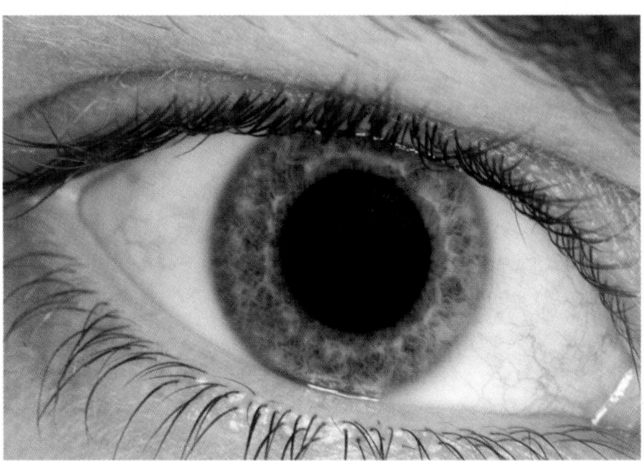

In dim light, the larger pupil lets in as much light as possible so that you can see more clearly.

TRY THIS! See how your pupils change

1 Look closely at your pupils in a mirror.

2 Now shut your eyes and slowly count to ten.

3 As soon as you open your eyes, look in the mirror again.

Did you see a difference in the size of your pupils? Your pupils should become smaller as they get used to the light.

Reflections

When light hits something that it cannot go through, it bounces off. Different types of surfaces make light bounce off in different ways.

Think about bouncing a ball. If you bounce a ball straight down on a smooth, shiny floor, the ball will bounce straight back to you every time. If you bounce a ball on an uneven surface it could bounce back in any direction! Light behaves in just the same way.

This glass and metal building shows a reflection of a nearby building in its surface.

When light bounces back evenly from a smooth surface, we see a **reflection**. A reflection is a picture of the object on another surface.

Mirrors, still water and shiny metals are all smooth surfaces. The smoother and shinier the surface, the clearer the reflection will be.

This deer is able to see its reflection in the surface of the water. →

Using mirrors

Mirrors that we use every day in our homes are usually flat. The reflection you see in them is the same as the object, but back-to-front. Try looking in a flat mirror. Wave with your right hand. Does your reflection wave its right hand or its left hand?

Some mirrors are curved. Car door mirrors are usually curved outwards. This gives a wide view, but everything looks smaller and further away than it really is.

This car door mirror is curved outwards.

Many things need mirrors to work. **Periscopes** use two flat mirrors. Light bounces off one mirror, down a tube and on to the next mirror, and then into your eye. This means that the image is passed to you using the mirrors.

The mirrors let you see over things that are out of view. When submarine crews are far below the surface of the sea they use a periscope to see what is happening above the water.

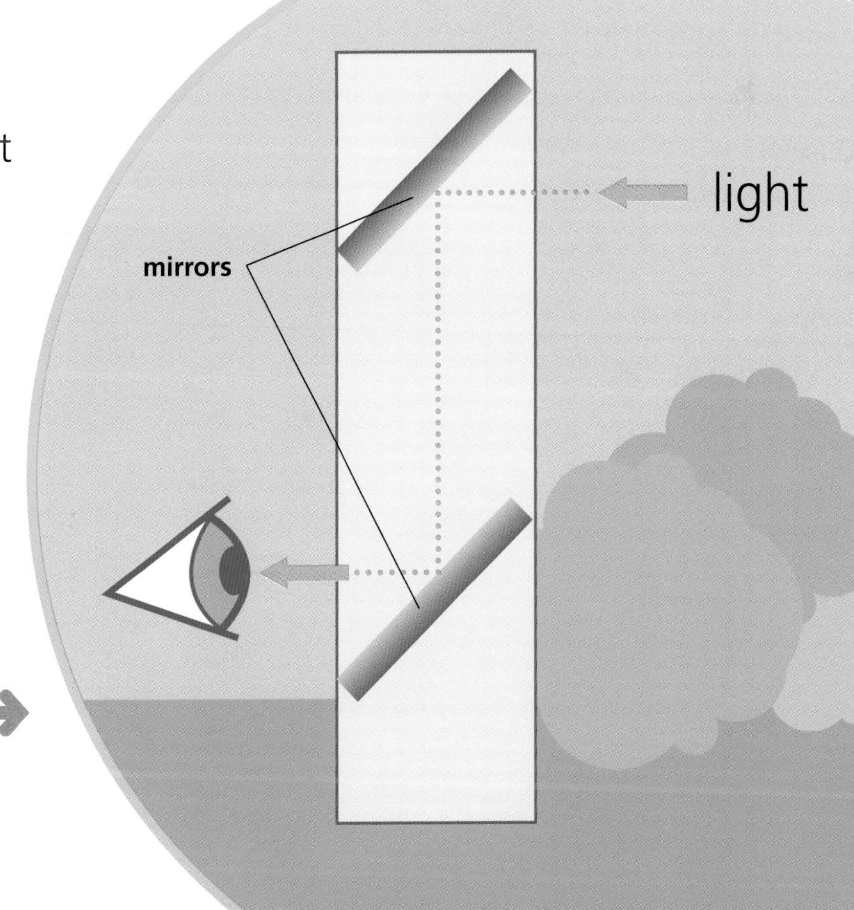

Periscopes use mirrors to see objects.

Bending light

Light rays travel in straight lines but sometimes they look bent. This happens when they travel from one thing into another.

When light bends in this way it is called **refraction**. It happens because light travels at different speeds in different things. For example, light travels more quickly through air than glass.

This girl's fingers look bent because of the refraction of the light.

This pencil is not really bent – it just looks as if it is.

You can see this for yourself if you put a pencil in a glass of water. Look at the pencil at the surface of the water – does it look bent?

TRY THIS! See how water bends light

1. Draw an arrow on a piece of paper or card.
2. Hold it up behind a glass of water.
3. Look at the arrow through the water. Move the card backwards and forwards slowly.

What happens to the arrow? Does it change direction? Is there a point at which you see two arrowheads? Can you make the arrow disappear completely?

All of these things happen because of the way the water bends the light.

Using lenses

Lenses are made of transparent materials, such as glass or plastic. They all bend light – but different shaped lenses bend light in different ways. An **optician** can give people glasses and contact lenses. These lenses bend light to help people see more clearly.

Some lenses are shaped to help people see things in the distance. Others are shaped to help people see things close to them.

An optician can test a person's eyes to see if they need help with their sight.

There are many types of lenses. **Magnifying glasses** bend light outwards. When you look through them, everything you see looks bigger than it really is. Telescopes use lenses to make things that are faraway look bigger.

TRY THIS! Make a magnifying glass

1 Put some water in a transparent container. Stand it on top of a newspaper or magazine.

2 Carefully put a drop of cooking oil on the water.

3 Look through the cooking oil. Does the writing look bigger through this?

The oil behaves as a lens and magnifies the writing.

Rainbows and colours

Sunlight appears white to the eye but it is really made up of seven different colours. A scientist called Isaac Newton made this discovery when he let sunlight shine through a wedge of glass, called a **prism**. A common way to see these colours is in a rainbow.

The colours of the rainbow are red, orange, yellow, green, blue, indigo and violet.

When sunlight shines through millions of raindrops, each raindrop acts as a tiny prism that splits the sunlight into colours. Together, all the raindrops make a rainbow in the sky.

TRY THIS! Turn colours into white

1. Carefully cut a circle out of card.
2. Divide the circle into seven equal segments.
3. Colour them in the order of the rainbow colours – red, orange, yellow, green, blue, indigo, violet.
4. Push a pencil through the centre.
5. Spin your pencil – and watch what happens to the colours in the circle!

You should find that the colours together look greyish-white when you spin the circle.

! **Take care using scissors**

Glossary

contract become tighter

cornea the clear covering of the eye

iris the coloured part of the eye

lens something that bends light

light source thing that gives out light

magnifying glasses lenses that make things look bigger than they are

man-made made by people

microscopes instruments that make small objects appear bigger

mirror shiny object that reflects light

opaque lets no light through

optician person who tests people's eyes

periscopes instruments for looking over tall objects

prism transaparent wedge of glass that bends light

pupil hole that lets light into the eye

reflection image formed when light bounces off a smooth surface

refraction when light travels from one thing into another

relax become looser

shadow a dark area formed when light is blocked off from it

telescopes instruments that make faraway objects appear closer

translucent lets some light through

transparent lets all light through

Further information

Books to read

Frightening Light by Nick Arnold, Horrible Science series, Scholastic Hippo, 1999

Light by David Burnie, DK Eyewitness Guides, Dorling Kindersley, 1998

Light and Dark by Chris Oxlade, Step-by-Step Science series, Franklin Watts Ltd, 2002

Light: From Sun and Bulbs by Chris Cooper, Science Answers series, Heinemann Library, 2004

Light and Dark by Peter D. Riley, Ways into Science series, Franklin Watts Ltd, 2001

My World of Science: Opaque and Transparent by Angela Royston, Heinemann Library, 2004

Light: Look Out! by Wendy Sadler, Science in your Life series, Raintree, 2005

Websites to visit

www.bbc.co.uk/education/dynamo/lab/make.shtml

Full of experiments you can do at home.

www.bbc.co.uk/schools/scienceclips

Lots of interesting information and quizzes to test your knowledge.

CD Roms to explore

Play and Learn: Science Experiments, Dorling Kindersley, 2000

Become a Science Explorer, Dorling Kindersley, 2000

Index